PLEASE REMIT
MY QUBITS

MARIE IRENE HINSON

the operating system
alter/altar print//document

PLEASE REMIT MY QUBITS

ISBN # 978-1-946031-83-9
copyright © 2020 by Marie Irene Hinson
with additional design, editorial and commentary by ELÆ
[Lynne DeSilva-Johnson]

This text was set in Europa, Minion Pro, Avenir, Franchise, and OCR-A Standard.

cover image uses: Villers, Marie Denise, *Marie Joséphine Charlotte du Val d'Ognes*. 1801. Oil on Canvas. Metropolitan Museum of Art, New York.

the operating system
www.theoperatingsystem.org
operator@theoperatingsystem.org

PLEASE REMIT
MY QUBITS

Acknowledgements:

Thank you to ELÆ [Lynne DeSilva-Johnson]for your generous instruction and all of the brilliant poets in the 2019 alter/altar writing workshop at Poets House.

CONTENTS

the point of origin,
the point of no return

SURVEY I

QUBIT	REMIT	PLOT	ACY
FOURIER	RANDOM	ORIGIN	SUPREME
SUBJECT	MINE	QUANTUM	SURVEY
DIVISION	LAND	TOWNSHIP	KING

QUBIT

about insides and outsides
the form it holds
what pushes back as
what pushes back as
what pushes back as
capitalism into
my body

REMIT

into my squishy insides
i know that what I've got to do is figure out a way to
get by
and then I want to share that way to get by with others
and to keep getting by with others
to come up with a word technology
that creates a vibrating, glowing, beautiful
boundary between that form of capitalism
and that form of me
unfortunately it feels like I'm getting to

PLOT

i'm looking for a technology
that lets me boil out the impurities
boil out the impurities
gives me back myself
i'm looking for a technology
that applies heat
the break and go
the constant fucking of my language
my shifty top bottom magic

ACY

of breath and wait
and breath and wait and move
of breath and wait and move
and weight into ground

FOURIER

staying close to
listening to
how capitalism talks
like how a tree talks
how our language talks
how our this is a job interview talks
how every interaction is like a job interview

RANDOM

what i'm curious about
is with how little i have
and we all have
that i came here carrying nothing
from across the sea
from across the dusty trail
that i came even with out a conscience
that i came to steal
that i came here carrying nothing
and looking to devour
i'm wondering what i do have
because i for sure
can't bend capitalism to a boil
bend that shit to a boil
bend that shit to a boil

ORIGIN

what draws the metal shavings out
of the wood and the rocks
is it image after image after image in rich description

SUPREME

is it saying
hey give me that?

SUBJECT

a capitalism landscape
i'm here
i'm here
i'm here
to extract my parts from
the capitalism landscape

i've died already
and that doesn't make me afraid

what i'd like to do now is walk away into other words
bigger words words with images
like reservoir
like reservoir
like mountain
like the clouds beyond the mountain

MINE

what i might be writing is a score for a dance
that hinges at
a point of cornice
of cornerstone
i might be writing a score for a dance

QUANTUM

i'm here for blood
i'm here for destruction
i'm here for power

SURVEY

more than i'm here for moving to the woods
because the ground under my feet and the trees above
my head
are a new york landscape
i like to say new york is an appalachian landscape
but appalachia is a new york landscape
a capitalism landscape
if i'd stayed
i'd still be living and breathing the same air
i'd still be seeing with the same eyes
and i don't have the patience to figure it out there in
the woods
everything gets sucked up to new york
nothing is anything but a new york landscape
i'm here because to be honest,
that aint my land

DIVISION

the way of extraction
using the tools of capitalism
to go get the parts of me that are part of its form
saying hay
hey!
Hey there.
give those back right now.

LAND

this way of living close too
buddying up to,
back stabbing maybe
becoming complicit in
marking my complicity
letting go of my guilt
feels more immediate and productive to me
than moving to the woods

TOWNSHIP

know what the boundary, what the shape
of capitalism is
this sounds silly to me
because I know it
I know it, i breathe it
i'm complicit in it
i make it over and over and over again
i kill for it
i'm complicit in its killing
i'm also not
what i'm trying to do is extract
myself from the capitalism body
by way of
by way of
by way of
documentation

KING

the way of
the way of
the way of
extraction

REMIT MY QUBITS

heirs to
benefit from
my desires

one by one
two by two
four by four

four by four
eight by eight
16 by 16

in frequent arrival
at an origin is
more than a dream

that i worry
m >> n
leads to the best

arithmetically
arriving
at the stop

the molecule
simulates
simulates itself

so that
when I come up
on the next grid

a state of origin
supreme
supremacy

please remit
my qubits into my body
so that i can touch them

until you
begin to
sweat with urgency

fit the last two
into one
mine is perfect

making the square
in the largest shapely-est
form there can be

i never know
what people
imagine me to be

grid of 40
frothing qubits
that can take 10,000

from the point where
sixteen folds
into one

grace with
my feet the
trace the boundary

in my blue
floral sweater
that pils up

mine the
steps
along the blocks

portal time
is polynomial
and i like

remain to
be walked
down past

to be sunk
in blue
flowers

possibility
loss
impossibility

bringing the goal
closer
to save my legs

watch
the best
play out

set on corners
the subject is
silver dust

of sufficient complexity
to be executed
by a nanometer wave

the vase of fake flowers
cut through
auto garage

mirror with its
face to the sky
blue flower sweater selfie

grids are
exhausting
an ask to fill

probably
is a range of
obstruction

the question
is a molecule
simulating itself

quick pace of
unstopping brilliance
on warehouse walls

given back
over to the setting sun
of the 8th and 5th

step onto
a court
gated around

for always
us
you never

SURVEY II

HEIR	PERPETUAL	FOR	EVER
CLASSICAL	FORTY-FIVE	HARD	LINE
WATCH	GRATITUDE	REPEAT	GRID
DESIRE	GRACE	PROBABLE	SECTION

HEIR

there's something to be said for the accumulation
for the documentation
the breaking down
over reaching
again and again and again

PERPETUAL

how to take care of myself
on the insides of this
on the insides of me
because the living is both
the inside and the outside

FOR

there's no simple math to make this happen
there's no simple math
a simple spell to
repeat
a simple spell to repeat
the first half like the second half
the second half like the first

when does the mirror break away
from its image
from the body that makes the image within it
the other half
the negative
the spell said a second time

the spell said with itself being named
so that it can be named and named and used again
and made over again.
the death spell the death spell the death spell

EVER

turn turn turn
like a rock a stone about its
axis in my hand

turn around
face this
put your face in this way

CLASSICAL

that is going to work for someone else
day after day after day after day
its not machine, it's what makes the machine run
turns it with the explosions of millions of years
millions of years of knowing words
hundreds of thousands of speaking words together

FORTY-FIVE

what is that part of me that i'm here to get back
that i'm here to make whole
what is that part of me that is the tools it takes to
make this world
that part of me that is the visioning force
that part of me that is complicit
that is deriving wealth
that is guarding its walls

HARD

look for the fearing and the letting go
repeat the spell
repeat the first half
the first half
the first half

LINE

being my bodily extraction from the world
from the rocks and the trees
the second half being this other extraction
of i don't know what
the other extraction of my hands
my tools, my words
the part of me that writes the world
that goes on and on and on
writing the world always
there's a part of me that is always
writing this world into being
what is that shape and form
that is outside of my body that
leaves me unwhole
unwhole

WATCH

how do i enact this spell
how do i enact this spell
how do i enact this spell
how do i enact this spell
how do i enact this spell

GRATITUDE

draw up close
draw up close
use the extractive tools
to place at the tip of your
tongue
the words for the spell

REPEAT

rise and fall of my breath
the death cult of words

GRID

the implosion
the falling down
the unravelling
the technology i use
circling back on itself
circling back on itself
collapsing under its own weight

DESIRE

what would it look like to get myself back from
capitalism
i don't know
i don't know
i mean it's already happened
where it fucked up is in the dying
in the annihilation of itself
the already dying
dying is the thing it doesn't have words for
that isn't a possibility.
decouple from that grief
not the grief of death itself
my body turning into worms
my body turning into this landscape
my landscape of bodies
not in the loss of someone
the grief of losing someone
i want to say over and over again
this is not what i mean

GRACE

losing
the afterlife
i'm hell bent
that's why i'm hell bent
to not trade in my life and death for
the life and death of capitalism
that is
that is
that is
to say
to say to say
that i want to extract
to make my own form aside
from the life and death of capitalism
another form
because there's more
there's more there's more
there's more there's more
sometimes its just got to be said directly
so there's something to be said
for the

PROBABLE

the living is both the inside and
the outside and the needs don't go away
to make some money to have some food, to have a
home
to be comfortable to be loved
to live in community
to have a soul

SECTION

the project is everything and nothing
everything and nothing to make it to the end
how do we feel whole when the whole is not complete

ABSTRACT / EXTRACT

1. Please remit my qubits. Please let go of those parts of me that are working for and with capitalism. Please remit to my body my ability to use my language and imagination to set off into and bring into being a future. A spell, a hex.

2. I moved to NYC in July of 2019. Two weeks in, I went to the Met where I saw the painting I used for the cover image by Marie Denise Villers. The artist in the white dress pauses from her easel to return the gaze of the viewer. Seeing and creating both. The energy fascinated me — familiar, magical, powerful, a putting together of all the pieces. I felt like I'd finally arrived in a place that I'd been traveling to for a long time.

3. My ability to move beyond my body and understanding saved my life. Dissociation is a survival spell. I grew up in a conservative evangelical community in rural Appalachia where I had no words for being whole as a trans and queer person. After I moved to Philly, I came out and felt the healing of getting back those parts of me that I didn't think existed, that were tied up in gender or a fundamentalist spirituality.

4. I wrote these poems in ELÆ's alter/altar II workshop at Poets House in late fall of 2019. In the workshop, myself and a brilliant cohort of writers, immersed ourselves in a multi-dimensional and interdisciplinary exploration of process. What all can a poem be? Everything! It can be whole! It can reach beyond. It can be a spell.

5. So after a few months of living in the city, I was really missing my community and family in Philly while working too much for too little money. I was exhausted and struggling to pay my rent. I'd always lived under capitalism but now I felt the quality of living right next to its source. Why had I given up so much

to be here? Why did I pick this of all places? How do I rest, how do I learn, how do I make my art, how do I have community? How is my labor, my migration, my imaginative power used for, necessary, and complicit in capitalism?

6. These poems explore these questions and movements from this moment of crisis and fear. I'm writing in a way that reminds myself that the whole and embodied contains the multi-vocal and fractured — my new spell for living under capitalism. I drew from ongoing research around my origin myths, starting with the 1606 and 1785 ordinances that set my migration in motion via my historical family. These violent spells provided the system for handing over immense wealth to my white ancestors. A grid for extracting people from place, calling it space and creating capital.

7. At the same time I was writing, google announced it had achieved quantum supremacy. Basically, it made a computer, a processor, built on the emergent boiling of the universe — randomness/imagination. This quantum computer, in 200 seconds, did the work that would take 10,000 years of conventional supercomputing power. I couldn't think of a better symbol of this contemporary stage of overwhelm. The language for describing the moment also felt like an eerie bookend to my origins. A white supremacy over space leading or building to a supremacy over time, or even the underlying ability to simulate these both into being.

8. This hex/book happens at this site of time, place, body, and many more things. I want to unextract and collapse. These poems incite the poles of origin myths and future simulations into resonance through the material of my writing, my body, my spell making, and my imaginative power. The idea is to listen to those resonances, consider what parts of me are resonating with them, to get those parts back. To make whole.

SOURCES

FIRST VIRGINIA CHARTER 1606

source: https://avalon.law.yale.edu/17th_century/va01.asp

Defined land rights for English colonists seizing land from people living on the east coast at the a year before first permanent settlement of the English in 1607 at Jamestown. The land was divided into two huge swaths — one given to the London Company, the other two the Plymouth company. These two companies would be responsible for finding settlers and spreading them out over the land to secure it and begin deriving wealth from it.

"between eight and thirty Degrees of the said Latitude, and five and forty Degrees of the same Latitude; And that they shall have all the Lands, Soils, Grounds, Havens, Ports, Rivers, Mines, Minerals, Woods, Marshes, Waters, Fishings, Commodities, and Hereditaments, whatsoever, from the first Seat of their Plantation and Habitation by the Space of fifty like English Miles, as is aforesaid, all alongst the said Coasts of Virginia and al raerica towards the West and Southwest, or towards the South, as the Coast lyeth, and all the Islands within one hundred Miles, directly over against the said Sea Coast."

LAND ORDINANCE OF 1785

source: https://www.loc.gov/item/90898224/

The newly formed version of what would be the United States Government set out its goals for territorial expansion based on an abstract grid laid over it's imagined future land. This ordinance picked up where the English charters left off, setting out into the land west of the Appalachians. The grid provided the framework for the rooting of white settlers. The abstract form implied a blank canvas, the genocide and removal of people whose land it was. This is how white america came to be. The handing over of other's wealth for free. Free wealth is what set western European migration in motion. This is what brought my historical family here.

Simply — the land was to be divided on north-south, and east-west lines into big squares first, called townships, of six miles by six miles. These would be divided into 36 smaller squares of one square mile each that could be sold or settled or further subdivided. The government's goal was to extend this grid to the Pacific Ocean.

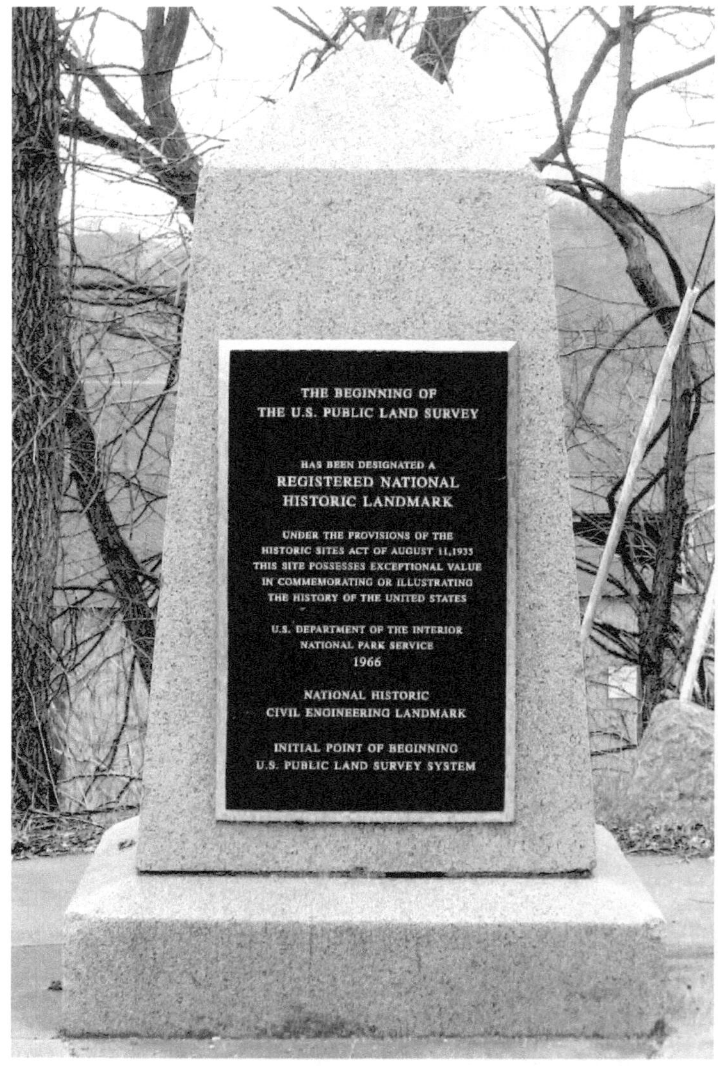

THE BEGINNING OF
THE U.S. PUBLIC LAND SURVEY

HAS BEEN DESIGNATED A
REGISTERED NATIONAL
HISTORIC LANDMARK

UNDER THE PROVISIONS OF THE
HISTORIC SITES ACT OF AUGUST 11, 1935
THIS SITE POSSESSES EXCEPTIONAL VALUE
IN COMMEMORATING OR ILLUSTRATING
THE HISTORY OF THE UNITED STATES

U.S. DEPARTMENT OF THE INTERIOR
NATIONAL PARK SERVICE
1966

NATIONAL HISTORIC
CIVIL ENGINEERING LANDMARK

INITIAL POINT OF BEGINNING
U.S. PUBLIC LAND SURVEY SYSTEM

POINT OF BEGINNING

source: https://npgallery.nps.gov/NRHP/GetAsset/
NHLS/66000606_text

This stone marker was placed to reference the point where the abstract grid first met the ground just three months after the passing of the Land Ordinance in 1785. Here was where the surveys began. Except, as the marker says the point is 1112 feet away, now under an artificial lake. The artificial lake was built in 1975 and is owned by FirstEnergy who had, as of 2015, dumped 80 billion gallons of coal ash into it.

"The Ordinance specified that the Geographer to the United States, Thomas Hutchins, would personally supervise the running of the first east-west base line; and on September 30, 1785, Hutchins began the Survey. As its beginning point he used the stake set by the Virginia Pennsylvania boundary commissioners. Hutchins proceeded westward until October 8 when, having surveyed less than four miles of the line, he suspended operations because of the threat of Indian hostility. Surveying began again on August 9, 1786."

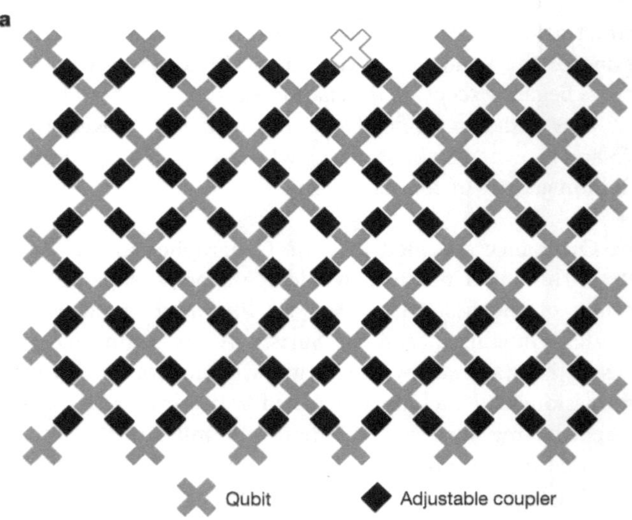

a, Layout of processor, showing a rectangular array of 54 qubits (grey), each connected to its four nearest neighbours with couplers (black). The inoperable qubit is outlined.

GOOGLE ACHIEVES QUANTUM SUPREMACY

sources: https://www.nytimes.com/2019/10/23/technology/quantum-computing-google.html
https://www.nature.com/articles/s41586-019-1666-5
https://www.scottaaronson.com/papers/quantumsupre.pdf

Quantum supremacy was achieved when a Google quantum computer did in 200 seconds of work what would take 10,000 years of work for a conventional super computer.

"The quantum supremacy experiment was run on a fully programmable 54-qubit processor named "Sycamore." It's comprised of a two-dimensional grid where each qubit is connected to four other qubits. As a consequence, the chip has enough connectivity that the qubit states quickly interact throughout the entire processor, making the overall state impossible to emulate efficiently with a classical computer."

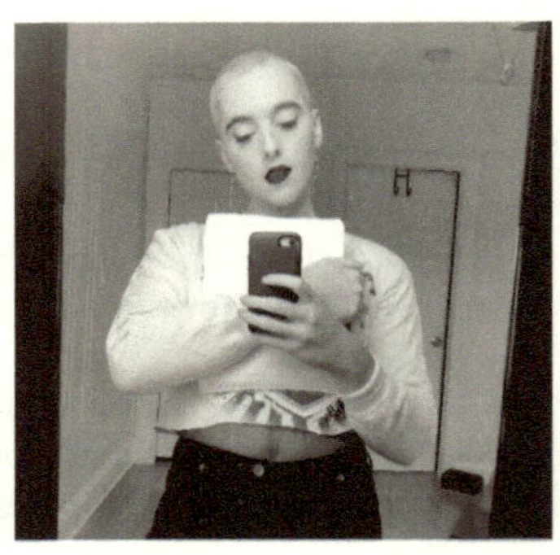

Marie Hinson is an artist practicing in film, writing, performance, and cinematography. Originally from the mountains of rural Appalachia, she now works and lives in New York City. She completed her MFA in Film at Temple University in 2013 and is an alum of the Philadelphia based artist collective Vox Populi. Her work has shown in a number of group exhibitions and experimental film festivals as well as at the Philadelphia Museum of Art, Anthology Film Archives, Scribe Video Center, Icebox Project Space, and Blackbox at Vox Populi.

mariehinson.com

WHY PRINT / DOCUMENT?

*The Operating System uses the language "print document" to differentiate from the book-object as part of our mission to distinguish the act of documentation-in-book-FORM from the act of publishing as a backwards-facing replication of the book's agentive *role* as it may have appeared the last several centuries of its history. Ultimately, I approach the book as TECHNOLOGY: one of a variety of printed documents (in this case,* bound*) that humans have invented and in turn used to archive and disseminate ideas, beliefs, stories, and other evidence of production.*

Ownership and use of printing presses and access to (or restriction of printed materials) has long been a site of struggle, related in many ways to revolutionary activity and the fight for civil rights and free speech all over the world. While (in many countries) the contemporary quotidian landscape has indeed drastically shifted in its access to platforms for sharing information and in the widespread ability to "publish" digitally, even with extremely limited resources, the importance of publication on physical media has not diminished. In fact, this may be the most critical time in recent history for activist groups, artists, and others to insist upon learning, establishing, and encouraging personal and community documentation practices. Hear me out.

With The OS's print endeavors I wanted to open up a conversation about this: the ultimately radical, transgressive act of creating PRINT /DOCUMENTATION in the digital age. It's a question of the archive, and of history: who gets to tell the story, and what evidence of our life, our behaviors, our experiences are we leaving behind? We can know little to nothing about the future into which we're leaving an unprecedentedly digital document trail — but we can be assured that publications, government agencies, museums, schools, and other institutional powers that be will continue to leave BOTH a digital and print version of their production for the official record. Will we?

As a (rogue) anthropologist and long time academic, I can easily pull up many accounts about how lives, behaviors, experiences — how THE STORY of a time or place — was pieced together using the deep study of correspondence, notebooks, and other physical documents which are no longer the norm in many lives and practices. As we move our creative behaviors towards digital note taking, and even audio and video, what can we predict about future technology that is in any way assuring that our stories will be accurately told – or told at all? How will we leave these things for the record?

In these documents we say:
WE WERE HERE, WE EXISTED, WE HAVE A DIFFERENT STORY

- Elæ [Lynne DeSilva-Johnson], Founder/Creative Director
THE OPERATING SYSTEM, Brooklyn NY 2018

DOC U MENT
/däkyəmənt/

First meant "instruction" or "evidence," whether written or not.

noun - a piece of written, printed, or electronic matter that provides information or evidence or that serves as an official record
verb - record (something) in written, photographic, or other form
synonyms - paper - deed - record - writing - act - instrument

[*Middle English, precept, from Old French, from Latin documentum, example, proof, from docre, to teach; see dek- in Indo-European roots.*]

Who is responsible for the manufacture of value?

Based on what supercilious ontology have we landed in a space
where we vie against other creative people in vain pursuit of the fleeting credibilities
of the scarcity economy, rather than freely collaborating
and sharing openly with each other in ecstatic celebration of MAKING?

While we understand and acknowledge the economic pressures and fear-mongering
that threatens to dominate and crush the creative impulse, we also believe that
now more than ever we have the tools to relinquish agency via cooperative means,
fueled by the fires of the Open Source Movement.

**Looking out across the invisible vistas of that rhizomatic parallel country
we can begin to see our community beyond constraints, in the place
where intention meets resilient, proactive, collaborative organization.**

Here is a document born of that belief, sown purely of imagination and will.
When we document we assert. We print to make real, to reify our being there.
When we do so with mindful intention to address our process, to open our work to others,
to create beauty in words in space, to respect and acknowledge the strength of the page we
now hold physical, a thing in our hand, we remind ourselves that, like Dorothy:
we had the power all along, my dears.

THE PRINT! DOCUMENT SERIES
is a project of
the trouble with bartleby
in collaboration with
the operating system